PHO COOKBOOK

MAIN COURSE – Step-by-step PHO recipes, quick and easy to prepare at home in under 60 minutes

TABLE OF CONTENTS

BREAKFAST 7

PHO BREAKFAST 7

ITALIAN BEEF PHO 9

PHO BAC 11

SHRIMP PHO 13

PHO GA 15

PHO 17

BEEF PHO 19

SOUP RECIPES 22

PHO BO – VIETNAMESE BEEF NOODLE SOUP 22

SLOWCOOKER VIETNAMESE NOODLE SOUP 24

PHO – HANOI NOODLE SOUP WITH CHICKEN 26

VIETNAMESE PHO SOUP 28

EASY PHO SOUP 30

SALAD RECIPES 33

VIETNAMESE NOODLE SALAD 33

SHRIMP MANGO SPINACH SALAD 35

PHO – COCONUT STEAK AND NOODLE SALAD 37

RICE NOODLE SALAD 39

VIETNAMESE PHO SALAD 41

ASIAN NOODLE SALAD 43

RICE NOODLE SALAD WITH SHRIMP 45

PHO SALAD 47

PHO SALAD 49

CURRY COCONUT STEAK AND NOODLE SALAD 51

- DIFFERENT PHO RECIPES 54
- EASY VEGAN PHO 54
- PHO 56
- VIETNAMESE CHICKEN PHO 58
- PHO WITH ENOKI MUSHROOMS 60
- VIETNAMESE HAPA PHO 62
- PHO SPIDE DUC CONFIT 64
- PHO WIH CHICKEN AND BOY CHOY 66
- MIDDLE EASTERN BOWL 68
- PAN FRIED TOFU 70

Copyright 2018 by Noah Jerris - All rights reserved.

This document is geared towards providing exact and reliable information in regards to the topic and issue covered. The publication is sold with the idea that the publisher is not required to render accounting, officially permitted, or otherwise, qualified services. If advice is necessary, legal or professional, a practiced individual in the profession should be ordered.

- From a Declaration of Principles which was accepted and approved equally by a Committee of the American Bar Association and a Committee of Publishers and Associations.

In no way is it legal to reproduce, duplicate, or transmit any part of this document in either electronic means or in printed format. Recording of this publication is strictly prohibited and any storage of this document is not allowed unless with written permission from the publisher. All rights reserved.

The information provided herein is stated to be truthful and consistent, in that any liability, in terms of inattention or otherwise, by any usage or abuse of any policies, processes, or directions contained within is the solitary and utter responsibility of the recipient reader. Under no circumstances will any legal responsibility or blame be held against the publisher for any reparation, damages, or monetary loss due to the information herein, either directly or indirectly.

Respective authors own all copyrights not held by the publisher.

The information herein is offered for informational

purposes solely, and is universal as so. The presentation of the information is without contract or any type of guarantee assurance.

The trademarks that are used are without any consent, and the publication of the trademark is without permission or backing by the trademark owner. All trademarks and brands within this book are for clarifying purposes only and are the owned by the owners themselves, not affiliated with this document.

Introduction

PHO recipes for personal enjoyment but also for family enjoyment. You will love them for sure for how easy it is to prepare them.

BREAKFAST

PHO BREAKFAST

Serves: **8**

Prep Time: **10** Minutes

Cook Time: **70** Minutes

Total Time: **80** Minutes

INGREDIENTS

- 1 chicken
- salt
- ½ onion
- Sriracha sauce
- 2 lb. rice noodles
- 1 cup cilantro
- 3 scallions
- ½ cup lime juice
- 1 jalapeno
- ½ oz. thai rock sugar
- 1 cup fish sauce

DIRECTIONS

1. Place the chicken on a baking sheet and season with salt
2. Transfer chicken to a pot, add water and boil for 35-40 minutes
3. Transfer chicken to a cutting boards and let cool
4. Simmer for another 30-35 minutes, add salt, fish sauce, noodles and top with broth and chicken
5. Garnish with cilantro, scallions and onion
6. Stir in lime juice, jalapeno, fish sauce and pepper
7. When ready, remove from heat and serve

ITALIAN BEEF PHO

Serves: **4**

Prep Time: **10** Minutes

Cook Time: **30** Minutes

Total Time: **40** Minutes

INGREDIENTS

- 4 cups beef broth
- 1 cup porcini mushrooms
- 1 tablespoon seasoning
- 1 tsp basil
- 1 tsp oregano
- ½ tsp garlic powder
- ½ tsp onion powder
- 1 bay leaf
- 1 lbs. deli roast beef
- 1 cup baby spinach
- ½ cup parmesan cheese

DIRECTIONS

1. In a bowl add beef broth and boil, pour broth over porcini and set aside
2. Add herbs and boil for another 10-12 minutes
3. Add noodles and simmer until they are al dente
4. Remove the mushrooms and add porcini broth to the pan
5. Pour porcini into bowls and add spinach
6. Top with parmesan cheese and serve

PHO BAC

Serves: **6**
Prep Time: **10** Minutes
Cook Time: **180** Minutes
Total Time: **190** Minutes

INGREDIENTS

- 3 shallots
- 1 tablespoon rice vinegar
- 1 serrano chiles
- 2 lb. rice noodles
- 6 oz. beef sirloin
- 1 yellow onion
- 1 lb. boneless beef chuck
- ½ oz. scallops
- 2 tablespoons salt
- ½ cup fish sauce
- 6 scallion
- ½ cup cilantro leaves
- pepper
- 1-piece ginger

- 1 tsp fennel seeds
- 4-star anise
- 1 stick cinnamon
- 1 pod cardamom
- 4 beef leg bones

DIRECTIONS

1. Put shallots on a aluminum foil baking sheet and broil for 20 minutes
2. Heat fennel seeds, cinnamon, star anise and cardamom in a skillet over medium heat for 3-4 minutes and transfer to a bowl
3. Place bones in a pot and cover with water, boil for 4-5 minutes, add shallots, ginger, beef and bring to boil
4. Add spiced, salt and scallops and cook for 90 minutes
5. Transfer beef to a bowl and cool, cook broth for another 90 minutes, reduce heat and stir in fish sauce and scallion, mix with vinegar and chilles in a bowl and set aside
6. Over noodles pour boiling water and divide noodles between 6 bowl, top with beef, sirloin, onions, cilantro and season with pepper before serving

SHRIMP PHO

Serves: **6**
Prep Time: **10** Minutes
Cook Time: **30** Minutes
Total Time: **40** Minutes

INGREDIENTS

- 8 oz rice noodles
- 1 tsp coriander seeds
- 1 tsp sesame oil
- 1 tsl ginger root
- ½ tsp garlic paste
- 6 cups chicken broth
- 2 strips lemon peel
- 1 tablespoon soy sauce
- 1 tablespoon fish sauce
- 1 tablespoon lime juice
- 1 tablespoon hoisin sauce
- 1 tsp cinnamon
- 6 cups bok choy
- 1 lbs. shrimp

DIRECTIONS

1. Prepare noodles according to package indications
2. Toast coriander, peppercorns in a pan for 4-5 minutes and remove from heat
3. In a pot, warm sesame oil, add chili, ginger and garlic paste and stir for 1-2 minutes
4. Stir in chicken broth, fish sauce, lime juice, hoisin, cinnamon and spices, bring to boil and add shrimp and bok choy
5. Simmer for another 4-5 minutes, add salt or pepper if necessary
6. Divide rice noodles into bowls and serve with cilantro

PHO GA

Serves: **4**
Prep Time: **10** Minutes
Cook Time: **30** Minutes
Total Time: **40** Minutes

INGREDIENTS

- Banh pho noodles
- Bean sprouts
- Cooked chicken
- Crispy onions
- Hoisin sauce
- Red chillies
- Sriracha chili sauce
- Lemons
- Black pepper

CHICKEN Soup

- 1 kg chicken soup bones
- ½ lbs. minced pork
- 1 stick cinnamon
- 3 pcs. Star anise

- 5 pcs. Cloves
- 1 tablespoons peppercorns
- 3 pcs cardamom pods
- 1 onion
- 5 cloves garlic
- 1 tablespoon palm sugar
- fish sauce

DIRECTIONS

1. In a pot sauté onion, garlic and cook on low heat
2. Add star anise, cardamom, cinnamon, sugar and stir well
3. Add water and boil for 1-2 hours
4. In another pot add oil, minced pork, chicken meat and pour back in the soup stock, boil for 30-40 minutes
5. Add noodles in a bowl, top with chicken meat, fried onions and chili
6. Pour boiling broth over noodles and serve with lemon and hoisin sauce

PHO

Serves: **6**

Prep Time: **10** Minutes

Cook Time: **30** Minutes

Total Time: **40** Minutes

INGREDIENTS

- 5 oz. rice noodles
- 1 lime
- 1 cup snow peas
- 6 cups chicken broth
- 1 lbs. boneless chicken breast
- 1 cup carrots
- 1-piece ginger
- 1-star anise
- 2 cloves
- 1 red bell pepper
- 1 tablespoon lime juice
- ½ cup scallion
- 2 tablespoons cilantro
- 3 spring basil

DIRECTIONS

1. In a bowl add carrots, snow peas, noodles and divide among 4 bowls
2. Add star anise, cloves and broth in a large pot and boil for 4-5 minutes
3. Reduce heat, add chicken and simmer for another 4-5 minutes
4. Add bell pepper, lime juice and simmer with salt
5. Ladle into bowls and top with cilantro or basil

BEEF PHO

Serves: **4**

Prep Time: **10** Minutes

Cook Time: **60** Minutes

Total Time: **70** Minutes

INGREDIENTS

- 6 cups chicken stock
- 2-pieces star anise
- 2-pieces cinnamon bark
- ½ cup fish sauce
- ½ lbs. beef
- 1/2 cup basil leaves
- 1 handful cilantro leaves
- 1 red chili pepper
- 1 lime
- sriracha sauce
- 2 stalks lemongrass
- 2 cups rice noodles
- 1 cup bean sprouts

DIRECTIONS

1. In a pot place stock, fish sauce, star anise, cinnamon, lemongrass and boil, lower the heat and simmer
2. Add beef slices in boiling broth and cook for 2-3 minutes, set aside
3. Divided noodles into bowls, add broth, bean sprouts, cilantro, basil leaves, chilies, beef and serve with lime wedges and hoisin sauce

SOUP RECIPES

PHO BO – VIETNAMESE BEEF NOODLE SOUP

Serves: **4**
Prep Time: **10** Minutes
Cook Time: **240** Minutes
Total Time: **250** Minutes

INGREDIENTS

- 3 lbs. beef bones
- ½ lbs. beef
- 1 onion
- 1 2-inch piece ginger
- 9 star anise
- 5 cloves
- 1 stick cinnamon
- 1 tsp peppercorns
- ½ cup fish sauce
- 1 tablespoon palm sugar
- 6 ounces rice noodles
- ½ lbs. pound steak

- 1 cup beans prouts
- ½ cup Thai Basil
- ½ cup cilantro
- 1 jalapeno peppers
- 1 lime
- 1 tablespoon hoisin sauce
- 1 tablespoon chil sauce

DIRECTIONS

1. In a pot add bones and fill with clean water
2. Add ginger, star anise, onion, beef, cinnamon, cloves, peppercorns, fish sauce, sugar and simmer for 2 hours
3. Remove beef and simmer for another 2 hours
4. Strain the solids and season with fish sauce, divide beef between 4-6 bowls, add noodles, beef and beansprouts
5. Garnish with basil, cilantro, jalapeno, lime slices, chili sauce and hoisin sauce

SLOWCOOKER VIETNAMESE NOODLE SOUP

Serves: **4**

Prep Time: **10** Minutes

Cook Time: **30** Minutes

Total Time: **40** Minutes

INGREDIENTS

- 1 whole chicken
- 1 whole onion
- 2 piece of ginger
- 2 tablespoons coriander seeds
- 2 whole cloves
- 2 whole star anise
- 2 tablespoons sugar
- 2 tablespoons fish sauce
- 1 lb. rice noodles
- 1 bag bean sprouts
- 1 handful cilantro
- 2 spring green onion
- sriracha sauce
- hoisin sauce

- lime
- 1 jalapeno
- pepper

DIRECTIONS

1. In a show cooker place, the chicken and add cover with water, add onion sugar, ginger, fish sauce
2. Wrap coriander seeds, cloves, star anise in cheese cloth, tie tight before adding broth, cook for 6-7 hours
3. Once finished, remove chicken and set aside
4. Prepare rice noodles according to the package directions
5. In a soup bowl add noodle, chicken, ladle broth into bowl and top with onion, green onion and cilantro, top with basil leaves, bean sprouts, jalapeno sliced and squeeze lime juice
6. Drizzle with Sriracha sauce and hoisin sauce

PHO – HANOI NOODLE SOUP WITH CHICKEN

Serves: **6**

Prep Time: **10** Minutes

Cook Time: **40** Minutes

Total Time: **50** Minutes

INGREDIENTS

- 6 cups chicken stock
- 2 tablespoons ginger
- 2 cloves garlic
- ½ cup cilantro
- ½ cup mint leaves
- 2 chicken breasts
- 1 lb. bok choy
- ½ lb bahn pho(Vietnamese rice noodles)
- 2 tablespoons scallion
- 3 oz. baby tatsoi
- Tuong ot toi(Vietnamese sauce)

DIRECTIONS

1. In a pot add chicken stock and bring to boil, add garlic, ginger, cilantro, chicken and mint leaves
2. Simmer for 25-30 minutes
3. Remove chicken and and let it cool, cut into small pieces and return to the pot, add bok choy and simmer for 10-12 minutes
4. Soak noodles, and cook them in boiling water until tender
5. Divide noodles into bowls, add scallions, chicken cilantro and totsoi, pour broth, bok choy and serve with Vietnamese sauce

VIETNAMESE PHO SOUP

Serves: **4**

Prep Time: **10** Minutes

Cook Time: **30** Minutes

Total Time: **40** Minutes

INGREDIENTS

- 6 cups beef broth
- 3 cup water
- 1 onion
- 3 cloves garlic
- 2 whole star anise
- 2 cloves
- 1 knob ginger
- 1 cinnamon stick
- salt
- 1 package pho rice noodles
- 10-ounces steak
- cilantro

DIRECTIONS

1. In a stockpot add onion, garlic, star anise, cloves, beef broth, water, cinnamon stick and bring to boil, simmer for 20-25 minutes
2. Cook the noodles according to the package, then cover with broth and stir in the steak
3. Top with cilantro and serve

EASY PHO SOUP

Serves: **4**

Prep Time: **10** Minutes

Cook Time: **30** Minutes

Total Time: **40** Minutes

INGREDIENTS

- 1 tsp canola oil
- 1 onion
- 1-piece ginger
- 2 cloves
- 1 cinnamon stick
- 1-quart beef broth
- 2 cups water
- 2-star anise
- 1 tsp sugar
- 1 tablespoons fish sauce

DIRECTIONS

1. In a pot add onion, oil, ginger, cinnamon and cook for 4-5 minutes
2. Add all ingredients for the broth and bring to boil, lower heat and simmer for 20-25 minutes
3. Cover rice noodles with water and soak for 10 minutes, discard cloves, cinnamon stick, star anise, ginger and onion
4. Divide noodles into bowls pour broth and add toppings

SALAD RECIPES

VIETNAMESE NOODLE SALAD

Serves: **4**
Prep Time: **10** Minutes

Cook Time: **30** Minutes

Total Time: **40** Minutes

INGREDIENTS

- ½ lbs. onion
- 2 handful basil
- 1 lime
- ½ smoked salmon fillet
- 2 carrots
- 1 cucumber
- 2 onions

DRESSING

- 2 tablespoons fish sauce
- ½ cup water
- ½ red chili
- 1 small lime

- 2 tablespoons sugar
- 2 tablespoons white vinegar

DIRECTIONS

1. Cook noodles according to the package, drain and rinse
2. In a bowl place all the salad ingredients
3. In another bowl mix all the dressing ingredients

SHRIMP MANGO SPINACH SALAD

Serves: **2**

Prep Time: **10** Minutes

Cook Time: **10** Minutes

Total Time: **20** Minutes

INGREDIENTS

- ½ cup white vinegar
- ½ cup olive oil
- 2 tablespoons water
- ½ tsp salt
- ½ tsp pepper
- ½ tsp honey
- ¼ pound shrimp
- 5-ounce spinach
- 3-ounces baby salad greens
- 2-whole large mangoes
- 1 cup pomegranate seeds
- 1 cup quinoa
- 1 cup walnuts
- ½ cup cheese

DIRECTIONS

1. In a bowl mix all salad ingredients
2. Serve when ready

PHO – COCONUT STEAK AND NOODLE SALAD

Serves: 2
Prep Time: 10 Minutes
Cook Time: 10 Minutes
Total Time: 20 Minutes

INGREDIENTS

- 4-ounces rice flour noodles
- 2 tablespoons curry paste
- 1 cup coconut milk
- ½ cup cilantro
- zest
- ½ tsp salt
- ½ tsp pepper
- 1 lbs. beef
- 2 scallions
- 2 carrots
- 1 cucumber
- mint

DIRECTIONS

1. Cook noodles according to the package
2. In a bowl mix all salad ingredients and refrigerate
3. Transfer the steak to a roasting pan and rub with the the curry mixture
4. Grill the steak and transfer to a plate
5. On a platter arrange noodles, carrots, cucumbers, scallion and steak, drizzle sauce over salad and sprinkle with cilantro

RICE NOODLE SALAD

Serves: **2**

Prep Time: **10** Minutes

Cook Time: **10** Minutes

Total Time: **20** Minutes

INGREDIENTS

- 8-ounces rice sticks
- 1 cup carrots
- ½ cup basil leaves
- ½ cup mint leaves
- ½ cup cilantro
- 5 tablespoons ketchup
- 2 tablespoons lime juice
- 2 tablespoons soy sauce
- 1 tsp Sriracha
- 6-ounces tempeh
- 1 tablespoon dry peanuts
- 2 tablespoons sesame oil
- ½ cup vegetable broth
- 5 garlic cloves

- 1 shallot
- 1 egg
- 1 cup bean sprouts
- 1 cup English cucumber
- 4 green onions

DIRECTIONS

1. Cook noodles according to package indications
2. Mix broth with sesame oil, ketchup, lime juice, soy sauce
3. In a skillet oil over medium heat, add tempeh and fry for 2-3 minutes
4. Add shallots, garlic and cook until shallots are soft
5. Add soy sauce and bring to boil, add bean sprouts, noodles and toss to coat
6. Remove from heat and top with cucumber and basil leaves, cilantro and peanuts

VIETNAMESE PHO SALAD

Serves: **2**

Prep Time: **10** Minutes

Cook Time: **10** Minutes

Total Time: **20** Minutes

INGREDIENTS

- ¾ lbs. steak
- 1 cup beef stock
- ½ onion
- 1 slice ginger
- 1 garlic clove
- 1-star anise
- ¼ lbs. rice noodles
- 1 Lebanese cucumber
- ½ lbs. coleslaw mix
- handful bean shoots
- ½ cup mint
- juice from 1 lime
- 1 tablespoon fish sauce
- ½ tsp chili flakes

- 1 tsp malt syrup

DIRECTIONS

3. In a bowl mix all salad ingredients
4. Serve when ready

ASIAN NOODLE SALAD

Serves: **4**

Prep Time: **10** Minutes

Cook Time: **10** Minutes

Total Time: **20** Minutes

INGREDIENTS

- 0.5 bunch broccoli rabe
- 0.5 onion
- 2 cucumbers
- 1 tomato
- handful of mint
- 1 serrano chili pepper
- 6 ounces bah pho
- 6-ounces cheese
- vegetable oil

DRESSING

- 1 lime
- 1 tablespoon olive oil
- 1 tsp fish sauce
- 1 tablespoon sugar

DIRECTIONS

1. In a bowl boil broccoli rabe, remove and drain the broccoli rabe into an ice bath
2. In a bowl add cucumbers, onion, tomato, cilantro and chili
3. In another bowl mix all dressing ingredients
4. Boil the noodles until tender
5. On a place add vegetables, dressing and toss to coat
6. Top with fried halloumi and serve

RICE NOODLE SALAD WITH SHRIMP

Serves: 3
Prep Time: 10 Minutes
Cook Time: 10 Minutes
Total Time: 20 Minutes

INGREDIENTS

- ½ lb. pho noodles
- 1 tsp peanut oil
- 6 large shrimp
- ½ cup iceberg lettuce
- ½ cup shredded cucumber
- handful of mint
- carrot
- ½ cup scallions
- 2 tablespoons nuoc cham
- 2 tsp dry roasted peanuts

DIRECTIONS

1. In a bowl soak noodles for 15 minutes and them drain them
2. In a pot bring water to boil and cook noodles for 3-5 minutes
3. In a frying pan sauté the shrimp for 1-2 minutes on each side
4. In a bowl add cucumber, lint, lettuce, carrot, scallions and noodles, top with shrimp and pour nuoc cham and toss well
5. Sprinkle peanuts and serve

PHO SALAD

Serves: 2

Prep Time: 10 Minutes

Cook Time: 10 Minutes

Total Time: 20 Minutes

INGREDIENTS

- 3-ounces bahn pho
- 4 ounces sliced beef
- 1-ounce red onion
- 2 lbs. bean sprouts
- 1 tablespoon lime juice
- 1 tsp fish sauce
- ½ tsp Chinese spice powder
- chili peppers
- 1 handful cilantro
- 1 handful thai basil
- 1 tablespoon vegetable oil
- 1 tablespoon hoisin sauce

DIRECTIONS

1. For dressing mix lime juice, fish sauce, vegetable oil, fish sauce and spice powder
2. In a pot boil water and add noodles, cook for 2-3 minutes and transfer to a strainer
3. In a bow add onion, bean sprouts, noodles, basil cilantro and beef
4. Pour dressing over and toss to coat

PHO SALAD

Serves: **4**

Prep Time: **10** Minutes

Cook Time: **10** Minutes

Total Time: **20** Minutes

INGREDIENTS

- 3 ounces bahn pho
- 1 tablespoon oil
- 1 tablespoon hoisin sauce
- 1 tablespoon lime juice
- 1 tablespoon fish sauce
- ½ tsp Chinese spice powder
- 4 ounces sliced beef
- 1-ounce onion
- 1 handful cilantro
- 1 handful thai basil
- picked chili peppers

DIRECTIONS

1. Soak the bah pho in water for 40-50 minutes
2. In a bowl mix all ingredients for the dressing: vegetable oil, lime juice, spice powder, fish sauce and hoisin sauce
3. In a pot add water and bring to boil, add the noodles and cook until tender
4. Add the sliced beef in the pot, when the beef is done stop cooking and drain the beef
5. Add to a bowl together with onion, bean sprouts, basil and cilantro
6. Pour the dressing over and toss to coat

CURRY COCONUT STEAK AND NOODLE SALAD

Serves: 2

Prep Time: 10 Minutes

Cook Time: 10 Minutes

Total Time: 20 Minutes

INGREDIENTS

- 5-ounces rice-flour noodles
- 2 tablespoons curry paste
- 1 cup coconut milk
- ½ cup cilantro
- zest and juice of 1 lime
- ½ tsp salt
- ½ tsp black pepper
- 1 lbs. beef sirloin fillet
- 2 scallion
- 2 carrots
- 1 cucumber
- 1 tablespoon peanuts
- handful of mint

DIRECTIONS

1. Cook noodles according to the package
2. Mix coconut milk, cilantro, lime zest, salt, pepper and curry paste in a bowl and mix well
3. Transfer steak to a roasting pan and rub with curry mixture
4. Grill steak and mix everything on a place, drizzle with sauce and serve

DIFFERENT PHO RECIPES

EASY VEGAN PHO

Serves: **4**

Prep Time: **10** Minutes

Cook Time: **30** Minutes

Total Time: **40** Minutes

INGREDIENTS

- 2-star anise
- 3-ounce shiitake mushrooms
- 1 tablespoon soy sauce
- 1 onion
- 3 cups vegetable broth
- 1 onion
- 1 garlic clove
- 1 2-inch piece of ginger
- 1 carrot
- 1 boy choy
- salt

- 1 clove
- 1 cinnamon stick

DIRECTIONS

1. In a pot add cloves, star anise, cinnamon stick and stir for 2-3 minutes
2. Add garlic, ginger, onion, vegetable broth and boil for 15-20 minutes
3. Add shiitake mushrooms, green onions, carrots, soy sauce and simmer for 10-12 minutes, add bok choy and simmer for another 2-3 minute or until tender
4. Divide the noodles into bowls and top with tofu or cilantro before serving

PHO

Serves: **4**

Prep Time: **10** Minutes

Cook Time: **30** Minutes

Total Time: **40** Minutes

INGREDIENTS

- 1 tsp canola oil
- 1-piece ginger
- 1 onion
- 5 cups beef broth
- 2-star anise
- 2 cloves
- 1 cinnamon stick
- 1 tablespoon fish sauce
- 1 tsp sugar
- black pepper
- 6-ounces flank steak
- 6-ounces rice noodles
- 2 scallion
- ½ bunch fresh mint

- 1 cup mung bean sprouts
- ½ dried thai chile

DIRECTIONS

1. In a pot boil water and in a saucepan heat oil over medium heat
2. In the saucepan add onion, ginger and sauté
3. In the pot add cinnamon, broth, cloves, anise and boil, cook for 12-15 minutes, strain both into a bowl, return broth to pan and sitr in sugar and fish sauce
4. Soak noodles in hot water for 15-20 minutes, add to boiling water for 1-2 minutes
5. Divide noodles into 4-5 soup bowls, slice beef and arrange over noodles
6. Ladle broth into bowls and top with scallion, mint or chilies

VIETNAMESE CHICKEN PHO

Serves: **4**

Prep Time: **10** Minutes

Cook Time: **40** Minutes

Total Time: **50** Minutes

INGREDIENTS

- 4-quarts water
- 1 tablespoon salt
- 2 lbs. chicken bone
- 1 whole chicken
- 2 –star anise
- 1 whole cardamom pods
- 1 tsp fennel seeds
- 1 tsp peppercorns
- 1 shallot
- 1 onion
- 1 tablespoon sugar

DIRECTIONS

1. In a stock pot add chicken bones, salt, whole chicken and boil for 25-30 minutes, when tender remove to a plate
2. In a iron skillet mix cardamom pods, fennel seeds, star anise, cinnamon stick and peppercorns and cook over low heat for 2-3 minutes, add spices to broth
3. In the same skillet cook shallots, onion and stir frequently for 5-6 minutes
4. Return the chicken skin and bones to the broth and bring to boil, add sugar and simmer or 25-30 minutes
5. Cook noodles in a saucepan for 5-10 minutes, drain the noodles and divide into serving bowls
6. Bring broth to boil and stir in chicken and cook for 2-3 minutes
7. Ladle the chicken and broth over the noodles and top with cilantro

PHO WITH ENOKI MUSHROOMS

Serves: **4**

Prep Time: **10** Minutes

Cook Time: **130** Minutes

Total Time: **140** Minutes

INGREDIENTS

- 2 whole cloves
- 2 whole star anise
- 1 cinnamon stick
- 1 cardamom pod
- 1 onion
- 1-ounce ginger
- 1 stalk lemongrass
- 2 l vegetable broth
- 1 lime
- ½ bunch cilantro
- 1 carrot
- ¼ lbs. rice noodles
- ¼ lbs. enoki mushrooms
- ¼ lbs. bean sprouts

DIRECTIONS

1. In a pan add cardamom, cloves, cinnamon anise and cook over medium heat
2. In a pot add oil, ginger, lemongrass, onion and fry for 4-5 minutes
3. Add broth, spices and boil for 2 hours
4. In a pot boil the noodles, remove and drain the noodles
5. Put all ingredients into bowls, squeeze lime juice on top and serve

VIETNAMESE HAPA PHO

Serves: **4**

Prep Time: **10** Minutes

Cook Time: **30** Minutes

Total Time: **40** Minutes

INGREDIENTS

- 2 onions
- 1 piece of ginger
- 5 lbs. beef bones
- 1 lbs. oxtail
- 4-quarts water
- ½ cup fish sauce
- 1 bay leaves
- 1 cinnamon stick
- 1 tablespoon peppercorns
- 2-piece star anise
- 6 cloves
- 2 tablespoons sugar
- salt

DIRECTIONS

1. In a stockpot add onion, ginger, oxtail, beef bones and cover with water, bring to boil and simmer on low heat for 90 minutes
2. Add bay leaf, star anise, peppercorns, fish sauce, cinnamon stick, sugar and simmer for another 90 hours
3. When ready, cool broth and refrigerate
4. For serving, soak pho noodles in a bowl, heat 4-quarts pot and add noodles, cook for 4-5 minutes
5. Ladle broth over meat and noodles and top with cilantro before serving

PHO SPIDE DUC CONFIT

Serves: **2**

Prep Time: **10** Minutes

Cook Time: **30** Minutes

Total Time: **40** Minutes

INGREDIENTS

- 1 tsp salt
- 1-star anise
- 1 clvoe
- 1 green cardamon pod
- 1 black cardamom pod
- ½ tsp fennel seeds
- ½ tsp coriander seed
- ½ tsp cinnamon
- ½ tsp garlic powder
- ½ tsp onion powder
- ½ tsp ginger
- ½ tsp cumin
- 2 duck legs
- ¾ lbs. duck fat

DIRECTIONS

1. Crush cardamom pods and remove seeds and toast them in a pan with fennel seeds, star anise, cloves, mix together with the rest of spices
2. Rub the spice mix over the duck and salt until completely covered and refrigerate for 12 hours
3. In a saucepan warm duck fat and pour over the duck legs, cook for 3 hours in the oven at 250 F
4. Remove the dock legs form the oven and let them cool, turn heat to 400 F and roast for 20 minutes or until crispy
5. Serve the duck legs wit salad

PHO WIH CHICKEN AND BOY CHOY

Serves: **4**

Prep Time: **10** Minutes

Cook Time: **30** Minutes

Total Time: **40** Minutes

INGREDIENTS

- 3 zucchini
- ½ cooked chicken from broth
- ½ onion
- 2 green onions
- ½ cup cilantro
- thai basil leaves

BROTH

- 1 tablespoon coriander seeds
- 2 cloves
- 1 yellow onion
- 6 cups water
- 1 whole chicken
- 1 fuji apple
- ½ cup cilantro springs

- 1 tablespoon salt
- ½ tablespoon fish sauce
- ginger

DIRECTIONS

1. Toss the coriander seeds and cloves in a pressure cooker
2. Pour 4 cups of water to stop the cooking process and add the chicken breast and cook until tender
3. Add cilantro, apple, salt and remaining water
4. Lock the lid and cook for another 15-16 minutes
5. Lower the heat and cook for another 15 minutes
6. When ready remove the lid and transfer the chicken to a bowl
7. Season the broth with fish sauce, salt, and cover with broth
8. Separate the meat from the breast and legs
9. Divide the zucchini noodles among 4 soup bowls, add boiling water, zucchini noodles and top with shredded chicken, ladle 2 cups broth into each bowl
10. Garnish with onion, basil, cilantro, and serve

MIDDLE EASTERN BOWL

Serves: **4**

Prep Time: **10** Minutes

Cook Time: **20** Minutes

Total Time: **30** Minutes

INGREDIENTS

- 1 eggplant
- ½ cup chickpeas
- ½ cup packed parsley
- 1 tablespoon nuts
- 1 tablespoon lemon juice
- ½ tsp oregano
- 10 cherry tomatoes
- 2 handful greens
- ½ cup lentils

DRESSING

- 1 clove garlic
- 1 tablespoon tahini
- 1 tablespoon water
- 1 tablespoon olive oil

- ½ cup lemon juice
- salt

DIRECTIONS

1. On a baking sheet add eggplant slices and mist them with olive oil and sprinkle with oregano and mint, broil for 8-10 minutes
2. In a bowl add greens, parsley, chickpeas, lemon juice and season with pepper
3. Remove from the oven eggplant and tomato when are done roasting and arrange them on top of the greens with lentils and chickpeas
4. Whisk together all ingredients for the dressing serve on the side

PAN FRIED TOFU

Serves: **4**

Prep Time: **10** Minutes

Cook Time: **20** Minutes

Total Time: **30** Minutes

INGREDIENTS

- 1 block firm tofu
- 1 tablespoon sesame oil
- 1 tablespoon soy sauce

DIRECTIONS

1. In a skillet add sesame oil over medium heat
2. Add tofu to the pan and stir occasionally
3. Once tofu is brown, add soy sauce and stir well
4. Add this to pho soup, salads and serve

THANK YOU FOR READING THIS BOOK!

Printed in Great Britain
by Amazon

47993996R00043